John Halifax, Gentleman

THE Department of Health will present further papers on School Hygiene at the General Meeting to be held at Saratoga, Sept. 5–8, 1876 Announcement of titles of such papers will be made shortly. You are cordially invited to be present, and assist in the discussions, and, if expecting to do so, will confer a favor by informing me Any comments on the statements of the present pamphlet will be welcome to us. Please address

D. F LINCOLN, M.D ,

8 Beacon Street, Boston

𝔄merican 𝔖ocial 𝔖cience 𝔄ssociation.

THE

HEALTH OF SCHOOLS:

PAPERS

READ BEFORE THE AMERICAN SOCIAL SCIENCE ASSOCIATION,
AT DETROIT, MAY, 1875.

YEARLY REPORT OF PROGRESS, *by the Secretary of the Department of Health.*
THE NERVOUS SYSTEM, AS AFFECTED BY SCHOOL LIFE, *by D. F. Lincoln, M.D.*
GYMNASTICS FOR SCHOOLS, *by J J. Putnam, M D.*
DEFECTS OF EYESIGHT AMONG AMERICAN SCHOOL CHILDREN, *by Cornelius R. Agnew, M D.*
RULES FOR THE CARE OF THE EYES, *by D. F. Lincoln, M D.*
MEDICAL INSPECTION OF PUBLIC SCHOOLS

REPRINTED FROM "THE JOURNAL OF SOCIAL SCIENCE," No VIII.

PUBLISHED FOR THE
AMERICAN SOCIAL SCIENCE ASSOCIATION,
BY A WILLIAMS & CO.,
283 WASHINGTON ST , BOSTON.
ALSO FOR SALE BY
G. P. PUTNAM'S SONS, NEW YORK   ROBERT CLARKE & CO , CINCINNATI
PORTER & COATES, PHILADELPHIA.
1876.

PROCEEDINGS OF THE DEPARTMENT OF HEALTH, AT DETROIT, MAY 11, 12, AND 13, 1875.

IN answer to a call issued from the Department, a public sectional meeting was held during the whole of the 12th and half of the 13th of May, at which were read completed and authorized reports from the committee of the Department, upon two subjects; viz., "The Nervous System as injuriously affected by Schools," and "School Gymnastics." Brief communications, made in response to an urgent public demand for information, were also presented by the Department, concerning Defects of Sight, the Care of the Eyes, Medical Supervision of Schools, Systematic Inspection of Schools, Statistics of Sanitary State of Schools, Statistics of Rate of Growth of School-Children, and School Architecture. The latter series of papers must be considered as provisory, rather than as containing the full expression of the Department's opinion. The Secretary's Report, explaining more fully the character of the work done, was read without debate, at the first general session of the Association, on the evening of May 11; and an abstract of it is here prefixed to the other papers: —

REPORT OF D. F. LINCOLN, M.D., SECRETARY OF THE DEPARTMENT OF HEALTH.

The report presented a year ago to the Association contained a summary of the plan then recently adopted by the Department, for studying school hygiene. It may be found in No. VII. of the Journal of the Association, printed September, 1874. Since then, the plan has undergone some slight modification. The following is the list of topics which the Department now intends to treat of: —

1. Heating and ventilation.
2. Light, and condition of the scholars' eyes.
3. Seats, and deformities traceable to them.
4. Architectural plans.
5. Apparatus employed in instruction.
6. Gymnastics.
7. Condition of the nervous system.
8. Condition of the organ of hearing.
9. Condition of the organs of pelvic cavity.

10. Drinking-water.
11. Sewerage and water-closets.
12. Commissions for sanitary inspection of given school districts.
13. Brief of a law establishing the office of medical inspector of schools.
14. Statistics of height and weight of school-children.
15. Contagious diseases in schools.

Of these, Nos. 6 and 7 are before you. Provisory reports upon Nos. 2, 4, 12, 13, 14, are also ready. Nos. 3, 8, 11, 15, are assigned to competent hands; while Nos. 1, 5, 9, 10, are not assigned.

Care has been taken, before presenting matter to the public, to secure it, as far as possible, from error in statement; to this end, we have been accustomed to criticise all papers, and to order their revision in accordance with such criticism as appears justified. This is usually done at the regular monthly meetings of the Department. Further criticism is expected through the press, and from private individuals; and, before an article finally takes its place in the Journal of the Association, it has undergone several revisals.

It is possible that the entire series of researches, which is not yet complete, nor perhaps will be for a year or two longer, will be published at last in a single volume, for popular use.

Attention is specially called to certain methods and formulæ, which have been used in several examinations of school-children, instituted within the past year, the results of which are to be presented at these sectional sessions.

(a) Those used in Philadelphia, during the past winter, under the orders of the Board of Control of Public Schools. These examinations are almost the first — certainly the first of any magnitude — ever carried out in the United States. The results have been partially tabulated; and a printed broad-sheet is ready, containing a great deal of information concerning the sanitary condition of the grammar schools in that city. But as the total number of separate reports is nearly four hundred, and there are many questions to be answered on each report, the labor of tabulating has been immense. It is fitting to add that the credit of organizing these measures is very greatly due to the Philadelphia Social Science Association, which we are honored in being permitted to call a branch of the American Social Science Association.

Similar investigations, with the same series of questions, have been set on foot in St Louis, by the public-school authorities; but no results have yet been published.

(b) Those used by Prof H. P. Bowditch in carrying out examinations of the height and weight of Boston public-school children, in accordance with the request of his department This is officially sanctioned by the school authorities; its execution will probably be a work of two years or more; and in its results it will furnish a contribution to the science of man, showing the present rate of growth of our native and foreign population at every period of life, from five up to eighteen years of age Such investigations, if they could be carried out in other parts of America, would prove of the utmost value, as furnishing a standard for comparing our populations with each other, and with those of Europe.

(c) Still another method of statistical research will be illustrated in the plans framed by Dr. C R Agnew of New York, a member of the Department of Health, who, in connection with others, has already examined the eyes of a great many school-children in Cincinnati, Brooklyn, and New York The result will show how many scholars of different ages in various cities have defective sight; and inferences of great importance will naturally spring from such observations. The same has been done, and is still doing, in St. Louis, Philadelphia, Albany, Rochester, and elsewhere Dr Hasket Derby, in Boston, intends to visit Amherst College every year, and examine the success-ive classes of young men, so that a just idea may be formed of the rate at which near-sightedness makes progress from year to year among a selected number of men at study. The continuous observations which he plans have a peculiar interest.

The secretary has also prepared, in outline, a set of rules for the care of the eyes, which will be read in connection with the above. Another outline has been drawn up by several members of the Department, for the purpose of bringing before the public the rules which architects ought to follow in build-ing schoolhouses, with a view to the health of their inmates The importance of having these points clearly understood by architects is extremely great; and I can hardly think of any subject connected with school hygiene, around which more interest would gather than around this, of " sanitary requirements of schoolhouses "

It is not yet possible to say what subjects will be ready for presentation at the next general meeting, but we hope to have ready more than one full report, with a great deal of statistical information (more or less incomplete) regarding the health of school-children.

The first session of the Department of Health was held in the Council committee-room of the City Hall, Rev. Charles H. Brigham of Ann Arbor presiding

The first paper was as follows : —

THE NERVOUS SYSTEM AS AFFECTED BY SCHOOL-LIFE.

BY DR. D. F. LINCOLN.   READ MAY 12, 1875.

You will not fail to be struck with the fact, which meets us at the very outset of our inquiry, that an intimate connection subsists between this subject and many others standing upon the list which has been drawn up to represent " School Hygiene."

This connection,.however, furnishes no obstacle to the execution of our plan of simultaneous joint authorship. Only one of the list covers ground belonging, in a strict sense, to the present investigation. That subject is the one alluded to under the title " Organs of the Pelvic Cavity," — a title designed to include all those derangements of health, about which so much has lately been written, occurring in young girls during the process of sexual development. About this matter I shall say very little, both because of my own want of special fitness for the task, and because it seemed to the department, that the time had not yet come when a judicially impartial account could be given of this subject which has of late aroused such bitter and general controversy. Perhaps in a year or two this may yet be done; but we have as yet made no attempt whatever to examine into the matter

The next difficulty, however, is one of far greater moment; and I may state it as follows : — '

Our entire nation is believed to be suffering from certain wide-spread sources of nervous degeneracy. Our children are but a part of the nation, and must suffer along with the older members of the population. How shall we discriminate between what is national, and what is simply scholastic? Give the child a constitution derived from excitable parents, a nutrition in infancy and childhood from which iron, lime, and the phosphates are mainly excluded; a diet in later childhood most abundant but most unwholesome, and based upon a national disregard of the true principles of cookery; a set of teeth which early fail to do their duty; a climate which, at its best, is extremely trying, killing either the aged by excessive cold, or the little children by a tropical heat; an atmosphere so deprived of moisture, that the most casual observers speak of it, and men of science consider it as capable of modifying our constitutions most profoundly ; add to these influences those of a moral nature, arising from the democratic constitution of our society, spurring on every man, woman, and child to indulgence in personal ambition, the desire to rise in society, to grow rich, to get office, to get every thing under the heavens; add a set of social habits, as applied to the life of young girls and boys, which is utterly atrocious, which robs so many of them of their childhood at the age of ten or twelve, and converts them to simpering, self-concious flirts, and men of the world, *rusés*, and independent of control, a depraved and pitiable breed of "little women and little men;" add finally the fact, that we have now a population of six millions dwelling in cities of over one hundred thousand inhabitants, and exposed to those deteriorating influences which notoriously belong to great cities: give the child these conditions to grow up under, and can you wonder that he or she "deviates from the type" (as it is fashionable to say) of the sturdy Anglo-Saxon pioneer who settled this continent? And can we wonder that educators, persons deeply interested in their profession, and sincerely conscientious, should protest against the charges brought by physicians against their systems of instruction, should protest against the very title of this paper, and should appeal from the laziness and folly of parents, and what they consider as the professional prejudices of medical men?

With these difficulties, inherent in the subject, you will pardon me, if I succeed in doing no more than positing the question. I nevertheless think that I shall show that schools do cause a certain amount of injury of the sort called "nervous;" but you must not look for any thing like a statistical exhibit of the *amount* of harm done. The method of investigation, which results in good statistics, has been cultivated in precisely this direction in several cities within the past year, as in Philadelphia, St. Louis, New York, and elsewhere; but the opportunities and the working-power of a single man are but very small, as compared with the amount that ought to be done even in a single city. The present paper therefore aims, first, to exhibit the physiological laws which govern the subject, and to show how school-life is capable on the one hand of benefiting, and on the other hand of injuring, the fabric called the Nervous System; and, second, to illustrate these principles by citations from the opinions and observations of about seventy persons, physicians, and teachers, who have favored me with correspondence.

PART I.

PHYSIOLOGICAL LAWS GOVERNING THE MENTAL AND NERVOUS HEALTH OF PUPILS.

In the most general terms, the nervous system may be characterized as an accumulator, a distributor, and a regulator of the forces of our animal economy.

By it the mind is informed of what may be seen, heard, felt, or touched; by it the perception is stored up, the thought remembered, the process of thinking carried on. By means of it, the beating of the heart, and the circulation of blood through the body, are regulated. If there is a demand for fresh blood, in order to sustain the activity of the brain, a portion of the nervous system is charged with seeing to it that fresh blood in greater quantities is sent to the brain. By means of nervous action, the tears flow, the mouth is moistened when we eat, the stomach is enabled to digest its food, and the bowels to carry on what the stomach begins. And by it, also, the muscles are enabled to act, and to transform chemical force into the forces of motion and heat. In fact, the muscular functions are in a sense nervous functions. Not only that nervous force is consumed in the performance of muscular acts, and is reciprocally strengthened by such performance, but also that the muscles themselves seem, in the ultimate analysis, to be simply a spreading-out of nerve-tubes, as the foliage of a tree is the expansion of its boughs and branches. Hence, when speaking of the department of medicine called neurology, or the special treatment of nervous diseases, we are obliged to include the diseases of the muscles themselves under the same heading.

I have not begun to exhaust the statement of the functions with which the nervous system is connected, but will just call your attention to the fact that every one of these relations is doubly reciprocal, like the effect of a pair of mirrors placed over against each other   Nothing happens to any organ which has not its effect upon some part of the nervous system; and nothing happens in our brains, or any other nervous organ, without producing its effect upon some organ not nervous

It is well to state here, in order to enable you to anticipate a little the results of this paper, that the actual derangements of the nervous functions which are commonly believed to be produced by improper influences at school are the following; viz, —

First, a group collectively termed "Neurasthenia," composed of debility and general depression, dyspepsia, sleeplessness, irritability, headache; then nosebleed, a symptom of congestion, which seems quite rare in America as compared with some parts of Europe; then chorea or St. Vitus's Dance, a disease of childhood proper; then neuralgia, hysteria, irritable spine, or spinal anæmia, and menstrual anomalies

This list was given in a printed circular of inquiry issued to physicians, and from their answers it appears that little remains to be added to the list. But I must add, that several correspondents have of their own accord suggested other evils of more or less importance; as insanity, self-abuse, injury to the urinary organs from long confinement, deformities of the chest and spine, and typhoid fever.

With this general view of the scope and tendency of our inquiry, let us now pass to the consideration of the question, " How may school influences directly benefit the nervous system ?"

In the first place, the school may provide for a reasonable degree of physical exercise, which every scholar should perform unless excused by his physician. There is very little chance for healthy sports in great cities; and it is precisely in these cities that the greatest number of hours is spent in schools   If civilization takes from its members the country air and country sports which are the natural means of health, civilization is bound to make good the loss to those who are too poor to make it good for themselves, and that means nine-tenths of the people in cities.

As regards fresh air, and other hygienic essentials of schools, the attempt is sometimes made to excuse deficiencies by saying that " the scholars are better off in school than in their own wretched houses."

This excuse is apt to prove fallacious. It is our duty to ask, when such remarks are made, "*How much* better off are they when in school ?" Is the air at home charged with fourteen parts of impurity, for example, and that in school with only twelve or thirteen parts ? Such a comparison reflects no credit upon the school : if both places are blamable, then our duty obviously begins at the school, which we build and furnish, and to which we compel the children to come :

But let us not delay over this sufficiently obvious point. What we desire to know just now is, whether a thoroughly good school is a positive benefit to physical health. Granting that the air is pure, and the surroundings are all hygienically perfect, are the work and the discipline of schools beneficial, *per se ?*

And first, as to the work, the simple mental work ; is that capable of doing positive good ?

The answer to this question is as follows: Pure mental work, quite free from what is called "feeling," is not possible to a conscious human being; but pure work, accompanied by the simple feeling of satisfaction termed "interest," in a moderate degree, acts on the system like any other healthy work, by consuming the chemical elements; if the brain is at work, one sort of change goes on ; if the muscles, another sort; but brain-work and muscle-work equally create a demand for fresh nourishment, and this demand constitutes a healthy appetite for food It is fully understood by "brain-workers," that certain studies tax the endurance of the entire system as much as the severest bodily toil. Persons with good brains are fatigued by mental labor as much as persons with good muscles are by bodily labor. Now, I do not mention fatigue as a desirable thing, but the processes which lead to fatigue are good if kept within reasonable bounds, and I hold it to be physiologically correct, that these processes are much alike, though not identical, in the acts of thinking and of muscular motion Indeed, voluntary muscular motion is absolutely dependent upon a supply of nervous force, which is probably generated in a portion of brain lying within the temples. When muscles are palsied, their nerves are pretty sure to be affected ; and when nerves, their muscles . hence it is often extremely difficult to say whether a given disease of either organ begins in nervous tissue or in muscular tissue.

Mental occupation, like all other natural occupation, is therefore good ; or, at least, it has a presumption in its favor. But the value of this work is vastly enhanced by the methodical way in which a good school enforces its performance. Our teachers, in many cases, deserve the greatest credit for their judicious firmness in restraining from overwork, as well as in requiring the full amount of work ; and I know well, that adult students would often be benefited by such regulations as would prevent them from over-driving their intellectual machine.

Why, then, can we not make our children work with their brains, and trust nature to develop their muscles? I believe there is a special reason why we may not do this, and somewhat as follows: The nervous organs require nutrition like other organs; they are dependent upon the blood, which conveys to them what is required to repair waste; and the blood is again dependent upon the heart and the blood-vessels, which pump it to the points of supply. Now, the heart and the blood-vessels are muscular organs; their capacity to force the nutritious fluid to its destination depends on the amount and the good condition of the muscular tissue they contain. A strong pulse is needed by a strong brain; and if we want a strong pulse we must strengthen the heart. And in no way can this be done except by muscular exercise, which drives the blood on to the heart, distending and stimulating it in such a manner that the organ gradually increases in size and firmness, growing vigorous in sympathy with the other muscles of the body. Of the danger of excess in this practice, I will speak later.

Of the muscular structures of the chest, there are some which have no particular use except to assist in breathing; these, the respiratory muscles, need a similar development through training, in order that pure air may be largely introduced into the lungs; a process which you know to be indispensable to the proper nutrition of the body, and the performance of the processes of oxidation required by all the tissues.

So far, we have seen that muscular activity is indispensable, even to the health of the brain; while, as regards the action of the brain in thinking, we have succeeded only in establishing a presumption in its favor. This being the case, — the one being essential, the other only permissible, — it would seem as if those who exercised their muscles stood a better chance of perfect health than mere brain-workers. It is commonly assumed, that boys are necessarily in better health when let run freely in the open air without schooling, and that day-laborers are the healthiest part of the community. But these assumptions are greatly neutralized by two facts, — the privations undergone by the poor, and the noxious effects, in any class or age, of excessive muscular exertion, which is certainly capable of doing as much harm as overwork of the mind. Consumption, various forms of heart-complaint, of palsy, of muscular disease, not to speak of the great enemy rheumatism, are the penalties of excessive muscular effort. Stupidity is another penalty, deserving serious mention.

The laboring classes have diseases as many and as serious as those of the intellectual classes. Nay, more: it would seem from statistics that the latter are much *longer-lived* than the former, however it may be with their health. Clergymen, lawyers, physicians, merchants, scientists, and men of letters live very much longer than the classes that work with their muscles chiefly; the figures are given differently by different authorities, ranging from fifty-six years up to sixty-five as the average length of life in the former, while the average life of all persons who reach the adult age is about fifty years. In the upper and professional classes in England, statistics relating to nearly forty-eight thousand persons have recently been published by Charles Ansell, showing that the average annual mortality in one thousand, of those under sixty years of age, was 10 46 as against an average of 17.65 for all classes in England and Wales

These figures may be taken for what they are worth · I use them only to rebut the common arguments in favor of the necessarily superior health of mere hand-workers But another turn is given to the argument by those who assume that the educated and the rich, though longer-lived, are more subject to chronic troubles, as dyspepsia, neuralgia, and gout. This view is most incorrect, I am sure, as regards the population of large cities. No one who has had experience in dispensaries can think that the poor have as good health as the well-to-do classes · The well-to-do are those whom Nature has blessed with tougher constitutions, greater powers of mental work and endurance ; persons of higher endowments in every way than those possessed by the poor hence, while they know better how take care of their health, they possess also better means for doing so Theirs are the sunny streets, the wholesome quarters ; while to the poor belongs the gift of large families, and a doubled or trebled rate of mortality in children. Hence also, permit me to say, upon them rests the imperative duty of helping their weaker neighbors to obtain a reasonable share of health and intelligence · The problem is, however, complicated, and it is impossible to give full value to all the arguments in this place.

So far we have seen, from several points of view, that the presumption is in favor of the wholesomeness of mental work, as required in a well-governed school. One reason for this has already been given It is good for the body, because it is bodily work ; because as such it furthers the processes of chemical transmutations, and hastens the renewal of tissue; and because it is better for us to have this renewal, a fresh body — one composed of recent elements — being more vigorous in all its functions than a stale and rusty organism This is the fact as it looks from a chemical point of view. But we scarcely need technical language in order to understand this It can be stated in every-day phrases; and it will be instructive to make a re-statement of this sort, which I will now do.

Our life is largely made up of appetites or cravings of various sorts

The most familiar of these are the cravings for food and drink, for breath, for sleep, for air and sunlight. The presence of any one of these, in a healthy person, shows the existence of a chemical exigency or crisis, which requires the addition of some element, — carbon, oxygen, nitrogen, fat, starch, animal fibre, salt, water, and so on; or the introduction of some force, as light, heat, or atmospheric electricity. If these desires are not gratified, the health suffers. Now, there is another class of cravings, equally important, and equally imperious in their claims : I mean the various desires to *expend* animal or mental force, — the longing to exert muscular energy, the desire to move about after having sat still for a long time. The entire range of our mental powers furnishes us with examples of a similar sort; as the gifts of speech, of laughter, of musical genius, of the power to observe, to paint, carve, or otherwise represent, the power to command other wills, the capacity for greatly loving other persons, for receiving or giving sympathy. All these must be exercised by those healthy human beings who possess them, under penalty of a loss of well-being.

Now, it is evidently impossible to exercise all our faculties at once in such a way as to bring each to a state of the utmost development. It is the business of an educator to see, first, that the faculties essential to well-being are developed, — the muscles of respiration, by singing, dancing, running, and childish athletic sports; the muscles of the will, by similar methods, and perhaps gymnastics; the intelligence, by school instruction of various sorts. But, while doing this, he should bear in mind those traits of childhood which are most irrepressible, and should both guide them and be guided by them. Muscularity — or more rightly expressed, a liberal indulgence in muscular sports — is the craving of healthy boyhood: if denied, no amount of mental occupation will take its place. On the contrary, mental stimuli are most dangerous to a boy who is physically idle, and only tend to hasten those sexual crises (so fatally ignored by many educators) which are sure to come, and to place a certain proportion in peril both of health and morals. I am speaking of a great evil, and one little understood; for which the remedies are to be found in a liberal stimulation of all the nobler parts of a boy's nature at once, — his will, his courage, his fortitude, his honor, his sense of duty to God and man, his interest in some mental pursuit.

As respects girls, there is no doubt that they are capable of taking as keen enjoyment as boys in muscular exercise, though of a somewhat different nature.

That it would be for their good to strengthen their wills and their courage by such methods, no physician can doubt. But the obstacles to such development are very great, especially in cities, and in all places where fashion imposes a limit to the expansion of the lungs, and cuts off the indulgence in the pleasure of breathing.

·I·trust enough has been said to direct your attention to muscular training;as a branch of education   But it would be a neglect of duty did I fail to add that the whole matter ·must; be under control and regulation, and that forced and violent exercises in gymnasiums, or out of them, are capable of doing great harm. It is a great mistake to work the brain till it can do no more, and then, feeling fagged out, to take violent gymnastic exercise or a long walk. Mothers know that their little boys *can* make themselves sick by playing too hard. Some children cannot play too hard, and some adults can be Hercules and Apollo in the same day: these are few. I would suggest, that a rule of the following sort be laid down for those who are old enough to follow it. " Never let the bodily exercise be so crowded into a corner by work that you cease to enjoy it, to relish it as a well person relishes food ; but, as to the amount of exercise you take, let that be governed by the appetite for it   And do not feel bound to make your biceps big; for the muscles which do not show —those lying between the ribs, under the shoulder-blade, and the diaphragm —̣ are more important, and are suitably developed by systematized breathing, by vigorous walking, and a little running or lifting, if you can bear it." Such advice is, on the whole, more judicious for adults, who have severe tasks of a mental nature, than would be the indiscriminate recommendation of gymnastics.

I come now to another set of causes, which ought favorably to influence the health of scholars   I refer to the fact, not much understood in a practical way, that *happiness* is of itself one of the surest sources of health , or, in medical terms, that joy is the best tonic we possess. Pleasurable sensations are imparted by all efforts made willingly, if within our powers. The scholar has that source of pleasure constantly, if he is well managed   He is interested; and interest is the chief factor in happiness, while want of interest is a sort of hell on earth. He has the sense of mastering difficulties, of conquering his own weakness and ignorance. His cheerfulness is promoted by making the work brisk and vigorous, both in recitation and during study. He is conscious of success and of gain, and that without reference to the standard of his fellows, but by reference to himself. His self-control and habits of order are strengthened; which must indirectly prove beneficial to his health. And, finally, he is conscious of having a friend and sympathizer in the person of his teacher , or, if not, there is serious fault to be found somewhere. Either the teacher is deficient, or else the class is so numerous that it is impossible for him to know the characters of his pupils.

Now let us turn the picture, and see the reverse. What *harm* is done through injudicious schooling?

In answer, let me say, that, if mental enjoyment does good to the system, the sensation of inadequacy to one's task is a source of acute suffering and injury. Pain felt in a nerve is a proof that the nerve is not duly nourished, or has been tired out by overwork; and, in accordance with this fact, we find that its proper function, that of distinguishing objects by means of touch, is weakened during an attack of neuralgia. In muscles, fatigue easily passes into pain, which may quite cripple one for a while, as when a person begins too violently with gymnastic exercises. But in the mind we feel the pain called depression of spirits, when required to discharge mental functions beyond our strength. The sensation is like that felt by insane patients suffering from Melancholia, to whom life is only a burden, and suicide the only apparent duty But it is rarely the case that such a condition occurs in young children. If overworked, their minds are apt also to be strongly interested, their feelings in a state of tension; their ambition acts as a spur, and does not let them know how tired they are; so that irritability, rather than depression, is characteristic of children suffering from school tasks. And be it said, that this state is most needlessly aggravated by a great many petty restrictions and points of discipline, which keep the child in a state of continual apprehension. He is perhaps marked for tardiness, and hence eats his meals in a state of trepidation lest he come late to school· he is marked for each recitation; he is constantly inquiring how he stands; and, if he is ambitious, the consciousness of impending destiny is ever present to his mind. I speak not of such folly as giving a child a demerit for not coming to school five minutes before the hour appointed; or giving merits for the performance of tasks like sweeping down the stairs of the schoolhouse, or sharpening the other children's slate-pencils! But we are called upon very strongly to condemn all points in the management of schools, which give rise to anxiety, apprehension; exaggerated feeling, in short, of any sort, whether of joy or pain, in the minds of scholars.

But leaving this point, and returning to the consideration of the effects of overwork: these effects are developed either by excess in quantity or by a monotonous strain of the faculties in one direction

As to excess in quantity, a child is capable of doing a good deal of work; but it must be done under the conditions of perfect sanitary surroundings, and, above all, of frequent rest. "The child's brain soon tires," says West, "and the arrangement, so convenient to parents, of morning lessons and afternoon play, works far less well for it than if the time were more equally divided between the two." The need of frequent recesses is admitted by all; but I find decided differences of opinion among teachers as to how frequent-they should be. If a child of eight or nine years works half an hour, he may be perfectly refreshed by five minutes' rest and amusement, and ready to go to work again; but, if he is kept at his tasks for four half-hours continuously, twenty minutes will not begin to suffice to bring him up to condition. A long unbroken session takes out of a young child more than he can make good by repair before the next session; and the total of these excesses of waste are subtracted from his total growth, stunting his body and mind together.

· Deprivation of sleep is another factor in producing exhaustion. And let it be remarked, that the worst thing about "home lessons" is the danger that they will be studied late in the evening, and, by the congested condition of the brain thus produced, prevent the child from falling into a sound, refreshing sleep

Deprivation of food often occurs. A child under twelve cannot usually go more than four hours without food, and privation of this sort, though willingly borne by the zealous scholar, makes itself felt at the next meal-time by an incapacity to relish or to digest what is set before him   Schools should always make reasonable provision of time and place for the scholars' luncheons, and, if there is a long session, parents ought to be expressly informed of this, and requested to furnish their children with something suitable   As for the regular meals, a parent is inexcusable who will permit a child to miss them, or to take them irregularly, or to lose its appetite for them, except in case of war, insurrection, or peril by sea

There is a condition, not infrequent in the adult occupants of schools in which a person seems to have used up all the surplus of vital force he possesses. There is no remedy for such cases but a protracted rest from all that can tax the powers.

The same condition may be observed in older children. But in the younger — say those under ten — the danger lies more in another direction. Educators, whether teachers or parents, are always liable to forget that the extreme volatility of a child cannot be conquered, but belongs to his nature; hence his tasks are always liable to be too monotonous — more like what an adult would think suitable than what a child would really be best suited with. Now, the overstraining of a faculty in any one direction is a most serious matter   If a clerk is kept too long at writing, the muscles which hold his pen grow weary; the weariness grows chronic; pain and constraint begin to be felt whenever he takes up his pen, one muscle gives out entirely, and he tries to make its place good by adopting a new plan of holding his pen; but the new way has again to be given up, and the entire process of writ-

ing soon becomes insupportable; he may even be prevented from work
by muscular spasms in the fingers. The remedy consists in three
things, — first, rest; second, treatment of the wearied muscles; and,
third, regular voluntary exercises of the other muscles — those which
are little or not at all affected — of the hand and arm   In other words,
the hand has to be drilled into a habit of distributing its forces among
various functions. The amount of mental and physical energy which
would carry a man easily through a day's work on a farm may thus, if
concentrated upon one set of muscular functions, set up a disease in the
latter, which will end in paralysis   Nor is this true of the hand alone.
A whole class of these diseases exists, denominated by the Germans
beschäftigungs-neurosen, or professional diseases. Thus the shoe-
maker's cramp, the ballet-dancer's cramp, the "hammer-palsy," of
sledge-hammer men, and the myalgia (muscular pains and debility) of
sewing-women

   We often hear a distinction made between "natural" and "unnatu-
ral" forms of bodily exercise; and the preference is instinctively given
to the former by most people. Now, the very best forms of natural
exercise are those which develop a rhythmic sequence of effort and
pause. Walking, dancing, and running never exercise the two
halves of the body at the same time in the same way; the efforts may
be constant, but they are relieved by alternations of right and left.
In fencing, the old masters try to teach a similar balance. It is not in
man's nature, when furnished with a pair of organs, right and left, to
use both at once in an absolutely identical way. Standing in a military position is the most fatiguing thing possible. And if we turn to
an organ like the eye, which is capable of severe labor of a more intellectual nature, we find that, though both retinæ are used together, yet
both take turns, at intervals, of resting, so that we actually, while
looking intently at an object, do lose sight of it, though unconsciously,
for a second, upon the right, and, presently, for a second, upon the left
side, and so on. Riding presents an instance where a pair of muscles
must be kept rather firmly and steadily stretched to clasp the saddle,
but, in riding, the whole body of the man is subjected to the rhythm of
another body, that of the horse, so that a multitude of unconscious
movements are made in the most perfect rhythm back and forward, to
right and left, by the trunk. I need not speak of the respiration, the
beat of the heart, the natural movements of digestion. Worshippers
in the true temple of Hygiea use for the most part an antiphonal
service; and the antiphony of effort and pause in mental operations
gives the most beautiful — as the Greeks would say, the most musical
— stimulus and expression to the mind

   We do not as yet realize how intellectual an organ a muscle is.

Those of the face are called mimetic, or muscles for the expression of emotion; but every voluntary muscle in the body, when in action, expresses the energy of one of the most complicated intellectual processes, though one little thought of as such, — that of volition. And I cannot refrain from tracing the analogy a step or two further, between the case of writers' palsy, and that of nervous excitability and exhaustion from severe tasks at school. The points of analogy are as follows the child's mental trouble shows itself by unreasonable behavior, fits of ill-temper quite foreign to his proper disposition; and the man's muscular trouble is commonly associated with strange and purposeless jerkings of the muscles, equally foreign to purpose and reason.

And, still further, if you observe a man trying to write in this disorder, you will see that the anxiety of the effort makes him ten times worse, as if his hand were afflicted with stuttering; while you well know that the anxieties arising from emulation, contention for prizes and rank, the unceasing effort to hold the tongue, to sit straight, to reach a given goal at a given time, wear out a child vastly more than long, hard lessons

I had thought to enlarge upon the latter point, but will rather leave it to my correspondents, from whom you shall presently hear expressions of opinion upon the matter

Although the subject of Diet is so essentially connected with Education, yet I must at present refrain from entering into a statement of the principles which should direct its regulation But upon one matter I feel specially called upon to speak. Modern Europe and America, during the last hundred years, have entered upon a vast physiological experiment. This consists in the use of a new order of stimulants, as a part of the daily life of everybody except very young children.

Whether in the energetic and strongly vitalized populations of the Western States, children are allowed the use of tea and coffee, I know not; but in New England it is extremely common among the poorer classes to allow these beverages in full strength, as an article of daily use, to children of five years old and upwards. Let me therefore explain my reasons for speaking of the latter custom, and (eventually) for condemning it.

Both coffee and tea act pretty much alike upon the system. In reasonable quantities they are capable of stimulating digestion, of relieving constipation, of counteracting in a remarkable manner the effects of severe cold, of relieving neuralgic headaches, of driving away the noxious sleep of opium and other drugs, and stimulating the mental faculties in an agreeable manner.

They seem to place the system in a condition in which more nervous force can be expended in a given time, so that the person can speak, think, walk, write, more vigorously and for a longer period. But, while thus laying a larger stock of ammunition ready to our hand, they also increase the danger of spontaneous explosions. While increasing our capacity for perceiving and feeling, they also render us more excitable; the feelings, whether of joy or pain, or of sentimental emotion, come quicker, and are more overpowering If they stimulate to muscular action, and render it more facile, they also give rise (as you all know) to occasional twitchings and tremblings of the muscles, quite annoying, and indicative of absolute excess in the use of the remedy.

In this respect, and in some others, there is a decided analogy between the action of these medicines, and that of *strychnia* taken in minute doses Animals poisoned with theine or caffeine die in violent convulsions. But the parallel is by no means complete. Rather let us say that these beverages act as *mobilizers of force.* To use them is like putting a hair-trigger upon your rifle.

I have not attempted to draw a picture of the evils which they may give rise to, but will confine myself to the legitimate inference which follows the last statements. If they render the expenditure of nervous force easier, in what tremendous danger may they not place the young and excitable minds of American children, eager to learn and to excel? If, under their influence, the teacher is enabled to sit up all night, attending to an excess of school-work, will not the scholar be driven by the pleasurable impulse to labor, and the conscious ease of action given through coffee or tea, to a degree of overwork, which, less in amount, may be equally disproportioned to his powers? I speak both of boys and of girls; but the latter will inevitably suffer more than boys. In the "grave, measured, and exact language of truth and verity," as Trousseau, the greatest of French therapeutists, phrases it, "Those whose nervous systems are weak suffer, when using coffee even in moderate quantities, from heat, anxiety, palpitation of the heart, sleeplessness; if they use it in excess, from headache, vertigo, tremor of the limbs, pusillanimity, eruptions on the face; it may give rise to or increase the diseases of hysteria and hypochondria." What teacher of children does not recognize this picture?

I desire, therefore, to express my wish, that the time may soon come when coffee and tea shall be withheld entirely from children under sixteen or eighteen years of age — according to their development — except when it is expressly recommended by physicians. It is absolutely beyond a question, that most children will develop a better physique without them. As for adults, their habits are necessarily very different from those of children, and we need not here extend our remarks to them. And, as beer and wine are scarcely used by children, I will also pass them by in silence

There are three special faults in sanitary conditions which do harm to the nervous system of those in schoolrooms. These are, the means employed in lighting evening schools, the undue heat of schoolrooms, and the excessive dryness of their atmosphere, with other impurities.

Our nation is fond of burning a good deal of gas or mineral oil, and as a result our rooms are apt to get overheated. One gas-burner consumes as much oxygen in an hour as several persons, thus contaminating the air very rapidly, and heating the upper strata very much. In burning, gas gives out impurities, very perceptible to the smell, chiefly composed of sulphurous acid gas; besides which, the power of direct radiation of heat possessed by a cluster of burners is very great; so that the heads of persons in the room, enveloped in a cloud of hot deoxydized sulphurated vapor, are subjected to the effects of radiant heat, which are of an irritating nature, quite different from those of fixed heat. Of course headaches and utter exhaustion are the result.

It is the general custom, I am sure, in American schoolhouses, to keep the thermometer at about 70° F., provided the furnaces will deliver heat enough. Dr Bowditch says: "In the sitting-room (of a family) the heat should not be above 72° F., nor below 68°; 70°, the medium, is the best." Now, with all possible respect for such high scientific authority, I beg to demur to this standard, widely accepted though I know it to be; for young persons and children, if properly fed and clothed and dried, it appears to me that 66° or 67° is quite enough. In the only perfectly ventilated schools I now remember, the temperature was kept at this point, and no complaint of cold was made by the scholars. The effects of excessive dry heat of climate upon persons of our race are usually manifested in the production of "simple general debility, a weakening of the bodily functions, marked by a diminution of the assimilative and digestive powers, and resulting in the loss of weight, and anæmia or poverty of the blood." And there is good reason to suppose that a difference of four or five degrees constitutes an important difference in climate. In an equable summer climate, a rise of the thermometer at noon to 76° may be felt, as an uncomfortable heat, while a fall to 68° will designate the day as "cool."

Neither heat, carbonic acid and oxide, sulphurous vapor, nor excessive dryness of the atmosphere, are felt as evils by the majority of our people; but all of them are dangerous in a special sense to the nervous system. Recent experiments made by Dr. Falk in Berlin show that air deprived of moisture makes the breathing more rapid and less deep; it quickens the pulse, and slightly lowers the temperature of the body; and in a few instances it appears that a current of absolutely dry air, continued for several hours, produced epileptic attacks in Guinea-pigs exposed to it. Dryness of atmosphere certainly tends to make the human subject irritable and excitable. A few people are the victims of untold misery when exposed to carbonic oxide fumes. I do not know what can be done absolutely to prevent the evil, unless we give up anthracite furnaces altogether.

PART II.

CITATIONS OF OPINIONS FROM PHYSICIANS AND TEACHERS.

In collecting opinions, it seemed best to address physicians in different terms from those used towards educators: two forms of circular, therefore, were employed. Thirty-four of the replies are from physicians, and forty-seven from principals of public or private schools, and superintendents of public instruction in various places. The information obtained from the replies has been arrayed under the following heads : —

1. Regarding the fact of the existence of these evils.
2. Nature of the maladies.
3. Excessive amount of study, as a cause.
4. Faulty methods of teaching, as a cause.
5. Bad sanitary condition of school, as a cause.
6. Dissipation out of school, as a cause.
7. The health of girls.
8. Health of teachers.

1. — *Existence of the Evils spoken of.*

[As regards this point, the question was put to physicians as follows : —
" Have you observed frequent injury (see below for definition) of a temporary or permanent sort, resulting from the excessive or unsuitable work exacted of children and young people in schools? "

This was answered affirmatively by twenty-two ; negatively by four ; "Yes but not from school-work proper," by four ; and, "Very rare with us," by one.

The corresponding question, put to teachers, read as folllows : —

" Have you seen pupils suffering from headache, nose-bleed, debility, languor, or other complaints, which you think caused by school-life or school-work? "

Answers : —

No 8
Rarely 18
Often 3
Yes 12

Total 41

By these the special remark was made, to wit, "Boys rarely," two ; "Girls no worse than boys," one ; "Never bad for the vigorous and strong," one ; "Yes, owing to bad food and lack of exercise," two ; "Yes, owing to over exertion in walking and gymnastics," two.

There is here a reasonable degree of agreement between medical opinion and that of professional educators (who for the sake of brevity shall be called "teachers") as to the existence of an evil; but medical men seem to be more impressed with its frequency than teachers.

2. — *Nature of the Maladies.*

That which may be called "Neurasthenia," characterized by the symptoms of debility and general depression, dyspepsia, sleeplessness, irritability, and headache, was mentioned by fourteen different physicians Seven others gave a general assent to the entire list of disorders printed in the circular and, of these twenty-one, several made special mention of the following diseases, viz,—

Menstrual anomalies 7
Irritable spine.... 5
Hysteria, chorea, neuralgia, each 4
Nose-bleed [1] . ...: ... 3

The following disorders, in addition to those named in the circular, were mentioned spontaneously, each by one or two physicians: Deformity of the chest or spine, injury to the urinary organs from long confinement in the school, phthisis (consumption), typhoid fever, self-abuse, insanity, of which only the last two properly come under the head of "nervous injuries."

The teachers' replies add nothing to this list.

3 — *Excessive Amount of Study, as a Cause*

As regards the actual amount of study required, it is stated by the teachers that the number of hours spent in school, inclusive of recitations, recess, and gymnastics, is reasonable in most cases, — twenty-five or twenty-six hours a week, or even less, in twenty-three cases; about thirty hours in ten cases; thirty-six in one; forty-five or fifty in one, and sixty in one. The two last are certainly very excessive, and this is admitted by the correspondents, who are principals of large academies in New England. Study at home is not required in nine cases; for scholars over thirteen years of age, two or more hours a day are required in eight cases, and less than two hours in fifteen; for those be tween ten and thirteen, one or two hours in seven cases, for those under ten, an hour a day in two cases. The latter requisition is certainly improper The amount of study was considered "suitable" by twenty-six teachers, while ten thought it too great in their own school or under their own observation.

4. — *Faulty Methods of Teaching, as a Cause*

A good many teachers have remarks to make pointing in this direction. The methods of teaching, and the qualifications of teachers, are spoken of in general

terms as inferior by 6
Emulation is condemned by 8
Emulation is praised by 3
Emulation is said to be good for boys by 1

[1] A symptom pointing to congestion of the head, observed frequently among school children by Guillaume in Neufchatel, and Becker in Darmstadt. In these American school-children it would seem to be less frequent. Of the "teachers," only three referred to it at all, though specially asked; and those three denied that they had ever observed it

The following recommendations are made, each by one or two teachers : —

To educate girls over fourteen as far as possible by themselves; to let young people over fifteen or sixteen study by themselves, to guard young children against the nervous excitement which arises from simple contact with a large number, even of the best scholars in a boarding-school, to let each young lady student have a separate sleeping-room; to inculcate religion as a motive for conduct; to give more frequent recesses; more play-ground; a room in the school for dancing in recess time, occasional reduction of work, or sending home for a while; to lengthen the terms, or require more time for the course of study, to pass the scholar more slowly through the different grades; to abolish public exhibitions; to abandon the "high-pressure" system; to give more prominence to the study of physiology; and finally "a total revolution !"

In fact, very few teachers have failed to see at least one point where the management of schools (I do not say of their own schools) is faulty; and physicians, in making their suggestions, have spoken particularly against those features of school life which tend to produce anxiety and worry, as competitions and public examinations.

5 — *Bad Sanitary Condition of Schools, as a Cause.*

Of these, ventilation is the only one mentioned by teachers, who speak of it as bad in various degrees in twenty cases, and as good in two.

6 — *Dissipation out of School, as a Cause.*

Question to teachers : "Do school-girls of fifteen and upwards spend much of their evenings in company or at public places of amusement? What kind of harm, and how much, do you think arises from this class of excitement as compared with school influences ? "

This class of excitement was said to do more harm than study by twenty-one; it was said by nine to do no special harm, in many cases because prohibited by the school; and twelve state that that the habit is frequent in the place they write from.

8[1]. — *Health of Teachers.*

A question put in the circular addressed to teachers was answered as follows : —

Health of teachers generally good, or no worse than that of other classes 5
Might be good if they took fresh air, &c. 2
Very unhealthy vocation if they do not obey the laws of health 2
Health generally poor 9
Not much better than that of sewing-girls 1
They break unless we take great care of them 1
More liable to break down than pupils 5
One of the occupations that bring most strain upon the nervous system 1
Health sooner affected than in other occupations 1

[1] For 7 see quotations on pages ~~101 110~~ 96

In conclusion, the following brief summary of the most conspicuous results of the investigation is presented · —

1 School-work, if performed in an unsuitable atmosphere, is peculiarly productive of nervous fatigue, irritability, and exhaustion.

2. By "unsuitable" is chiefly meant "close" air; or air that is hot enough to flush the face, or cold enough to chill the feet, or that is "burnt" or infected with noxious fumes of sulphur or carbonic oxide.

3. Very few schools are quite free from these faults

4. Anxiety and stress of mind, dependent mostly upon needless formalities in discipline, or unwise appeals to ambition, are capable of doing vast harm. It is hard to say how much is actually done, but a strong sentiment against such injudicious methods is observed to be springing up in the minds of teachers.

5. The amount of study required has not often been so great as would harm scholars whose health is otherwise well cared for.

6. Teachers who neglect exercise and the rules of health seem to be almost certain to become sickly, or to "break down."

7. Gymnastics are peculiarly needed by girls in large cities, but with the present fashion of dress gymnastics are impracticable for larger girls.

8. The health of girls at the period of the development of the menstrual function ought to be watched over with *unusual* care by persons possessed of tact, good judgment. and a personal knowledge of their characters.

9 One of the greatest sources of harm is found in circumstances lying outside of school-life. The social habits of many older children are equally inconsistent with good health and a good education.

EXTRACTS FROM CORRESPONDENCE.

From a Boston Physician — "I have not infrequently met cases of *consumption*, that could be *traced directly* to *over-stimulation* by examinations at the end of the school year. That is, the patients having kept up under inordinate strain during the term, made strong efforts to gain honors, and broke down immediately after, and when I saw them were far advanced in phthisis I have no doubt that confined and bad positions during study-hours, and want of exercise, had their influence, but that *over*-study was apparently the death-blow seemed evident I have seen so many of such cases, that I now urge parents who have transmitted frail constitutions to their children, or whose children from any cause are feeble, not to permit them to go but 'half-time,' to school, and to leave as soon as the health wavers in the least "

"Over stimulation of the brain undoubtedly produces all the symptoms you mention, each child being affected with that form of complaint to which, from personal and hereditary peculiarities, he or she may be especially liable. What I have said particularly applies to public schools, where but little or no allowance can be made for idiosyncrasies.

" Brain-work is constantly in excess of the capacity of the constitution to endure, and at the same time comply with the demands made upon it by other processes, such as growth, development, &c."

The above is quoted as a strong, and perhaps exceptional opinion, held by an eminent specialist. In contrast to it see the following from a late eminent teacher in the same city : —

From a Teacher in Boston —" During my fifty years in a schoolroom, I have seen no cases of ill-health, which, in my opinion, could be justly attributed to ' the school. True it is, that ' headaches, &c., are many times more numerous, now than they were fifty years ago ; but this does not result so much from the fact that boys are worse than then (although it is unquestionably true that the sources of corruption are far more numerous and wide-spread than formerly), as they do from the altered style of living in the better part of the community. Boys and girls are not born with the constitutions of their grandparents, and therefore they cannot endure so much."

" As far as my own direct observations are concerned, I could refer to many such evils as you speak of in the case of *teachers*, especially, or rather exclusively, among young women. . . I know of one case where there was some, but not a strong tendency to mental disease, inherited in a young girl of fifteen, who evidently broke down, lost a vigorous, elastic condition of health, and became ill with melancholia of a severe type, attended with delusions and some stupor, simply from *cruel* overwork to stand high in her class and ' pass the examinations ' "

" Yes · more especially have I observed these injuries resulting in young girls. I would likewise say, that, in addition to one or more of the symptoms which you enumerate, deformity, contracted chest, and distorted spine, are frequent results of overwork of the brain, combined with bad position and long-continued application."

2.

From a Massachusetts Physician. —" Through timidity and want of foresight, previous to entering school, the little children suffer from inattention to the calls of nature. I think female teachers are very careless respecting their children in this matter, and personally I have known great suffering in consequence. This long-continued confinement of young children, I consider to be a very great evil. I can see no propriety in confining these children more than a very brief period at one time."

A Grammar School. —" I have noticed irritability and languor among boys, caused, however, by self-abuse. The boys of the first class I always warn 'at the beginning of the school-year against this by no means uncommon evil. In classes lower, I do not hesitate to talk to boys individually when necessary. It is strange to me that parents, especially fathers, do not warn their boys against this vice in their early years Of the great number of boys I have talked with, I have found but two who had ever been warned ; and, in every instance (?) the vice has been learned at the early age of nine or ten years ; in one instance at the age of five years "

From a former Superintendent of an Insane Asylum —"I must answer you from recollection. I have had one case of typho-mania, three of acute mania, six or seven of delusional disorder and great prostration, of female teachers from Boston and vicinity. I have seen a few cases of hysteria, and one of epilepsy (female teachers), *all* manifestly from over-work and anxiety of teaching The epileptic was manifestly suffering from the bad air of the schoolroom, and has made a good recovery, i.e , no fits for four years.

3.

From a New England Normal School. — "The work done by students requires constant application of the mind five days each week, of nine or ten hours' study ; or from *forty-five* to *fifty* hours. I consider this too much. The ill effects of this pressure are obviated in good measure by, 1. Ten minutes' intermission each hour, with marching movements to and from recitation-rooms. 2 By constant appeals to the perceptive faculties, and use of apparatus in objective methods of teaching 3 By a regular daily exercise in light gymnastics in hall, with music, for at least thirty minutes at close of afternoon session, with marches and great variety of movements. 4. By short terms of ten weeks each, thirty weeks in school-year, with two weeks' intermission between terms. 5. By voluntary self-discipline, which in the main is all that is needed of this class [*Normal*] of pupils. My observation of these requirements leads me to say that for adult students, many of them teachers, five rather than seven hours are sufficient in the building . . . *Generally, almost invariably, those who keep the exercise retain their health and mental power.* Others, who do not exercise as enjoined, are more subject to irregular conditions of body and depression of mind under the discipline described above This is equally true of either sex."

5.

A Grammar School.—"The ventilation of most of our school-buildings is simply abominable And I do not believe it will ever be much better until School Boards, and not Common Councils, build these structures. The school-building in which I am is a 'modern' one, built three years ago It is impossible to keep the air from becoming unendurable in a very short time, except by opening the windows."

From a New York Physician —"One young gentleman (of most exemplary personal habits), who was studying hard for examination in a school of engineering where the curriculum was severe and the class-room mephitic, ran himself down into a condition of toxæmia and neurasthenia, which caused me some anxiety , and he informed me that several of his classmates had completely broken down under the same circumstances. In less degree, the consequences of excessive mental strain with insufficient exercise and ill-ventilated rooms are things of almost daily experience. The injury is probably due, not so much to the amount of mental work in ordinarily robust individuals, as to the conditions of inadequate arterialization under which the brain is forced to perform this work "

6.

From an Academy for Girls, New Hampshire. — "I feel that much social relaxation unfits the mind for the closest application. It sometimes takes a week to get over the effect of an evening out, with no great excitement. It affords topics of conversation on persons and things that do not tend to elevation, and the breaking up of the regular routine of study hours loosens the hold these hours had on the mind. One evil should be avoided. It is, parents and patrons sending for pupils to go home on special occasions, such as dancing-parties at their own houses, and then sending them back to school, dragged out and exhausted, nervous and unfit for study. Three weeks will sometimes pass before the effect of such a visit passes away."

From Calais, Maine. — "I have known, since 1869, while carefully watching fifteen hundred school-children in our schools, two girls injured by hard study. I have known more than five hundred injured by late hours and the excitements of social life, and more than fifty I can recall at this moment whom I know to have been seriously injured by late hours, party excitement, and premature introduction to social life."

7.

A Girls' Private School. — "It seems to me that among such scholars as I meet, the greatest difficulty lies in an incomplete adaptation to a changing phase of society. I mean, that, for the past twenty years the social, and what I should like to call the æsthetic, claims upon young girls have been constantly increasing, until they are incompatible with an amount of school-work that twenty years since did not seem unreasonable, and did not produce any bad results, so far as I may judge from the experience of my own contemporaries. Now, if all these outside claims are just and right, the school-demands must be in some way modified, of course, but if they are, as I think they will prove, excessive, they will yield in time; and, meanwhile, there must be such adaptation as is possible, and that mainly by individual effort. Then, when society recognizes that it should not expect from school-girls the artistic, musical, and dramatic experience of the accomplished woman of society; when the mothers of our girls can moderate the excited cravings of the inexperienced seeker of pleasure; and when their physicians will inquire what has kept the healthy girls and women from nervous and other complaints, then I believe that the demands of society, and parents and physicians, will entirely coincide with those of the school-teachers, and with the best good of the scholars."

A Seminary for Girls, New Hampshire. — "School influences upon growing girls of thirteen and upwards, so far as my observation has extended, have not been unfavorable to their development as women, nor injurious to their general health. I believe they should be carefully treated, and relieved from *oppressive* burdens and work, especially when they desire it, *at stated periods*, for a short time With this care, which cannot be so properly exercised in mixed as in separate schools, our young ladies may complete a full course of solid and ornamental study, and come out in full vigor of body and mind."

Principal of a' Boston High School. — " Not unfrequently I see girls suffering from headache or languor, which seems to me caused by the wear of school-life; not merely by the work, but by the anxiety, the restraint, and confinement, of school I have rarely seen boys of fair constitutions in our high school suffering from overwork, — not half a dozen cases in ten years. I have often noticed a great change in the appearance of girls after leaving school. Pale, thin faces grow fresh and plump in a few months It seems to me desirable that girls should be educated as far as possible after fourteen by themselves, and without any stimulus further than that furnished by their desire to have their teachers' approval. In an experience of eight years in a private school for girls, I found no other stimulus necessary. I think any kind of emulation among girls is morally and physically hurtful. With boys the effect is certainly different, and is on the whole good "

A Private School for Girls in Boston — " I have never made it an *arbitrary rule* to suspend or change the course of study, and with ordinary common-sense care with regard to clothing, and the surrounding pursuits and interests of life in young girlhood, there are but few who have not been able to be present and to do the usual amount of work. I think, as a general thing, I have observed keener nervous sensitiveness, and less concentration of thought perhaps, for the first year or so [of the period between fourteen and eighteen], but after this, if the rest of the nature has been developed healthily and wisely, I have usually found increased interest and power of comprehension and acquisition. . . I believe, that, even in exceptional cases, a moderate use of the intellectual faculties is of great benefit to mind and body "

A Physician in Boston. — " The male sex, at about the age of puberty and while fitting for it, need looking after quite as much as the female sex, so far as head-work is concerned. . . Both sexes, under circumstances, have the lessons to get out of school [in Boston], and sometimes, I believe, at the cost of brains as well as body in after years."

8.

Principal of a Boston High School. — " Female teachers have generally more than the average strength of constitution , but in our *mixed* schools there are few upon whom the worry of school teaching and discipline does not have a very marked effect."

Principal of a Boston Grammar School — " The young lady teachers are many of them fresh from school, and the continuous work soon causes the health to fail The practice recently inaugurated [in Boston] of exacting out-of-school work in perfecting themselves to teach special branches, has been a great tax upon their vitality."

A Boston Grammar School. — " A better chance to maintain good health than in any other calling open to the average class of women."

Superintendent of Schools, Springfield, Mass. — " School-teaching is very exhausting But most teachers are imprudent. If conscientious and ambitious, they over-work, and do not divert themselves sufficiently *out of school.* A worn-out teacher is used up for this world.   But the circumstances under which they work have more to do in producing ill health than the work itself. I cannot think the occupation, as such, particularly injurious.   It seems to me otherwise "

At the close of Dr. Lincoln's paper, the following paper was read by him in the absence of the author. —

GYMNASTICS FOR SCHOOLS.

By J. J. Putnam, M.D.   Read at Detroit, May 12, 1875.

For the purposes of this brief paper, which can claim to have a suggestive value only, I have thought it best, in considering the subject before us, to attempt to give answers as definitely as possible to the following three questions, which I think cover the points mainly at stake in the matter : —

1. In what way, and to what extent, may gymnastic training be made useful in the education of school-children ?

2. What means of securing it have been anywhere adopted, and with what results ?

3. What means would be likely to insure the best results in our own schools ?

The first question, as to the utility of gymnastic training for children in general, calls, perhaps, most of all for a definite answer ; for it would, I think, become evident to any one looking at all closely into the matter, as it certainly has to me, that the greatest obstacle to the general introduction into schools, of any satisfactory system of physical training, would be in the want of definite appreciation, on the part of both the public at large and of controllers of school education, of the proper and possible value and aims of such a system.   Those teachers are, I believe, in the minority, who regard the study of physical culture as something worthy of being pursued in schools with the same method and persistency that all are ready to accord to the training of the mind.   Many of them feel a certain jealousy lest what they consider as the highest branches of education should suffer by the introduction of this new and apparently less important study ; not remembering that the proper aim of school education should be to fit us in every possible way for the work of our after-lives   Let it but be shown, however, that physical training of such a kind as can be obtained to advantage only under the guidance of skilled instructors is an important part of this preparation, and its right to a place in the school, where alone such instruction can be had, must impress itself upon all by an irresistible logic. This done, the question as to what particular system would best be adopted in special cases would soon be settled, and for this, as for other branches of school education, competent teachers would soon be found.

I will here forestall the main objection made to the introduction of any system of gymnastic exercises into schools, — viz., that such exercises could never be as useful as play in the open air, — by calling attention to two points first, that however true this might be for children who were by nature strong, and inclined to follow outdoor sports, yet to those of whom a certain number are to be found in every school, who, if left to themselves, would take little or no exercise out of doors, — to these, at least, the influence of school gymnastics might make the difference of health instead of invalidism in after-life ; second, that in certain important respects the benefits to be expected from outdoor play and from systematic physical training are essentially different In the case of the latter, it is not so much the enforcement of a certain gross amount of general bodily exercise that would constitute its chief value, but rather the careful and scientific training of the various groups of muscles of the body, whether it be those concerned in carrying on the functions most necessary to life and health, as that of respiration, or those employed in walking, running, and standing erect

It is manifest that for ends like these the aid of skilled teachers and well-considered methods of instruction would be absolutely requisite. I shall then endeavor to show that systematic school exercises may be of service in the education of children, first by promoting general health, second by bestowing certain special and highly important accomplishments.

In discussing the possible benefit of school gymnastics to the general health, I believe it to be best to refer but little to physiological explanations and theories, the validity of which in some cases is still an open question, in order not to awaken in the minds of scientific and thoughtful persons a spirit of distrust rather than a spirit of confidence.

The relation between indiscriminate physical exercise and the general health is certainly not one of direct proportion With adults, at least, great muscular development is neither necessary nor directly conducive to good health, valuable as it may be indirectly or as an accomplishment. Athletes are by no means always among the healthiest persons; and, on the other hand, we can all recall within the circle of our own friends instances of the combination of perfect health with only moderate strength of limb It was commonly stated, during the late war, that the young men of the city were able to stand the hardships of campaign life better than their more muscular brothers from the country. I do not mean to under-estimate the immense value of great strength,

considered as an accomplishment merely; and still less would I under-
value its tendency to lead its owner into the open air, where other and
more essential elements of good health are to be found; nor would I
deny that with growing children the importance to the health, of a large
amount of outdoor exercise, may be comparatively greater than with
adults. I desire only to place in stronger relief the statement that,
even for children, systematic training, when properly directed, may be
of value to the health, although it may not involve any large amount
of physical exercise. One way in which it can be made pre-eminently
useful is by helping to perfect the all-important process of respiration.
That much needs to be done and can be done in this direction, was
shown to some extent in the case of the children of the Boston schools,
by Prof Monroe, during the few years of his successful teaching. It
seems, at first thought, as if the power of breathing properly were given
us, in most cases at least, already perfected by Nature; or, at all events,
as if its development were something beyond our own control. In fact,
however, this is far from true. The singing-master has to work hard
and long to enable his pupils to sustain a good tune through a few bars
of music; orators with fine voices are rare among us; and yet, with
the basis given by proper school-training, we could often perfect ourselves in these accomplishments by almost unconscious practice. The
power to do these things is not, to be sure, necessary to good health :
in fact, the conditions of good health (if by that be understood the
power of doing, without injury or suffering, the work which is required
of one) must vary with the habits of each individual, and for one leading a life of idleness they might dwindle to a minimum, so far as physical exercise is concerned; but the man or woman, in our average society,
whom a short hill or a flight of stairs obliges to slacken their pace for
want of breath, or whom an enforced run to the cars may seriously
injure, cannot be said to possess that degree of development of the
power of respiration that the conditions of health demand in their
case   The nervous processes involved in breathing properly are, indeed,
largely automatic in their character, but, in order that the complicated
machinery of the automaton shall work satisfactorily, it must first be
put in order; and to do this must be the work of the intelligence.
Nature is not a lavish giver, or only to the few; and any thing like
perfection in development, we must win for ourselves by careful study.
Furthermore, it is beyond question, that such systematic education of
the functions of respiration might, and often does, help to save one
endowed with less than the average power of resistance, from lingering
and fatal diseases of the lungs, — so much so that the practice of exercises in breathing, even in a crude form, is frequently prescribed by
physicians in the treatment of such cases.

The best treatise upon the proper method of educating the breathing powers and the voice, that I have been able to find, is the little book by Prof Monroe, whose name has already been mentioned. Most of the German and French works on gymnastics, with the exception of those treating of their use in disease, complete as they are in other respects, appear to be somewhat deficient in this. For the exercise recommended by Prof. Monroe, no apparatus or special costume is required For proper walking and running exercises, a large empty room would be almost essential.

A proper system of physical culture in schools would also have reference to healthful positions in sitting or standing, more or less directly connected with the general health, of which, however, I will not now speak, further than to say that in connection with the question of school desks, which is being studied by another member of this department, that of the best method of developing the muscles of the back will have, sooner or later, to be considered.

If it is concluded that our children, like our ancestors, should sit erect and unsupported while they study, their muscles should certainly be so trained that they should be able to do so with the least possible fatigue, and the least possible temptation to sink into slouching postures.

Apart from the relation between physical training and the general health under ordinary circumstances, there are certain injurious influences peculiar to school life, the effect of which the school is surely bound to neutralize so far as possible.

Chief among these influences are, first, that of continued study through several hours, in the course of which intelligent application is likely to degenerate into listless mental drifting; not to speak of the ill effects, especially upon the circulation of the blood, which attend sitting in one position for so long a time. I find that this is already well recognized by many teachers, as well as the advantage of breaking the morning session by a few moments of gymnastic exercise Second, that of the foul air, which in a schoolroom accumulates so rapidly, and of which, with our present insufficient means of ventilation, we are hardly able to get rid, except by a thorough opening of windows, during which process scholars would be liable to take cold if not fenced against it by active exercise. Third, improper positions in sitting, which give rise, with a frequency of which teachers are perhaps hardly aware, to deformities, which in after-life bring the scholars under the doctors' care. Thus I have it on good authority, that in a school of 731 pupils, at Neufchatel, 62 cases of deviation of the spinal column were observed among 350 boys, and 156 cases among 381 girls. These results are further stated not to differ materially from those of examinations made in German schools. According to Adams, in 83 per cent of 782 pupils in which this deviation occurred, it was towards the right, probably in consequence of writing at unsuitable desks According to Eulenburg, in 92 per cent of 300 cases the curvature was also to the right. It is true that these curvatures are not always associated with public health, since they sometimes occur in a slight degree to the strong and well; and it is true also, that they may arise under influences not peculiar to school life, such as the preponderating use of one or the other arm for any purpose. There can be but little doubt, however, that to the habit of writing at unsuitable desks belongs the largest share of blame

It will be noticed, that, in the statistics which I have just given, the spinal curvatures were found to occur with much greater frequency among girls than among boys, — partly due, no doubt, to the fact that they play fewer active games, and are in general more restrained in their movements. In the brief report of a recent meeting at Berlin, of some of the highest authorities of Germany, called together to consider the entire subject of the school education of girls, I find a notice of an address by Herr Raaz, principal of a school in Berlin, in which he speaks of the common occurrence of these spinal curvatures in his school, and says that he has found the use of gymnastics to be powerful in preventing them.

I may anticipate somewhat by mentioning that at the end of their meeting it was unanimously voted to be very desirable that the study of gymnastics should be introduced as an obligatory subject into the programme of instruction in schools for girls.

I cannot leave the subject of health-giving relations of judicious physical exercise, without calling attention to the fact that without it lectures on hygiene and physiology must lose one-half of their value. The scholar must have been made to feel the benefit and sense of satisfaction resulting from the proper use of his muscles before lectures on the subject can be turned by his brain into working influences Just as the artist's eye detects a slight blemish in a painting to which one less trained would be indifferent, or as a skilled musician shrinks at the sound of a false note, so one to whom the conditions of health have become practically familiar, whether it be good air to breathe, or the proper use of the muscles of the chest and back, is far more keenly sensitive to the failure of these conditions than he could possibly be if they had been known to him as intellectual conceptions merely

The systems of exercises which would meet the ends hitherto referred to may be found in various books upon gymnastics, many of which are known to you all. Most of these systems do not require a special hall, but only that there shall be room enough in the neighborhood of each desk — as a successful teacher writes — for the pupil to be able to take one step in each direction, and swing the arms freely in all directions. They may be used daily or even several times a day for a few months, for instance, immediately after a recitation ; as, indeed, is already done in some of our schools.

I should be glad to speak of the value of physical exercise regarded as an accomplishment in training the scholar in certain special respects The boy or girl who can climb and jump and run as they are taught to do in Swedish schools, and can do so better than his or her companions, has an advantage over them to be compared with that given by the power of speaking another tongue

A large hall, with a few simple pieces of apparatus, is all that would be needed for these exercises, and the instruction need be given but once or twice a week Such a hall is coming to be considered a *sine qua non* in the best common schools in Europe, so that Mr. Philbrick, late Superintendent of the Boston schools, on his return from a recent visit to Europe, writes that "in Vienna every modern schoolhouse has its gymnasium, and every school one or more gymnastic teachers, no special teachers in this branch being employed in the public schools in the city."

A third important work which its advocates say is done by gymnastic training in connection with school life consists in inculcating a sense of discipline and self-subordination in the minds of the scholars which serves to increase the efficiency of the school in its other departments.

On this point I shall not dwell, because, so far as I have found, no two opinions are entertained as to the reasonableness of the claim. Whatever else may be said about the desirability of having military drill in higher schools and colleges, no one, I think, acquainted with the subject, would hesitate to give it his support in this respect.

Leaving now the health and strength giving influence of physical culture, let us pass for a moment to not the least important of its relations ; viz., that in which it is directly associated with a more purely mental, or, more strictly speaking, artistic cultivation, keeping to the expression and thereby to the more perfect conception of feelings and emotions that are not sufficiently precise to be satisfactorily translated into words, but that need another language analogous to that of music. It is universally conceded, that the use of the art of sculpture in some of the nations of ancient Greece was due, among other causes, to the strong hold upon the people of that physical culture which in other respects was productive also of such wonderful results Even if not themselves practised orators and athletes, the artists of Greece lived surrounded by those who were such, and thus imbibed their spirit.

It is true that we strive to foster an artistic sense among our children by familiarizing them with the manifestations of grace and strength in the human form, in providing our schoolrooms with casts of ancient statues, &c.; but we forget that the artists who modelled them, and whose fine taste we hope to appreciate if not to acquire, must, to some extent at least, have derived their power to do so from observing men and women around them, with whom physical grace and the control of the body had been a matter of lifelong study; and partly, also, as the natural outgrowth of their own pursuit of physical culture. It is surely but natural, that the keen sense of appreciation, which only an expert can feel, of the exact meaning of this or that poise of the body, of the economy of power and the hidden strength implied in it, should help to awaken in the artistic mind the desire to embody these conceptions in durable forms.

To foster to any great extent the art of sculpture, may not lie in the province of the common school, any more than it is in its province to foster any other of the special accomplishments to any extent; but it certainly does belong to it, so far as possible, to prepare the soil in which such an accomplishment might grow. Furthermore we must remember, that these works of art are beautiful only because they represent the possibilities of human development, and that the thing itself should be of more importance in our estimation than its image.

Rev. Charles Kingsley in writing on this subject, after referring enthusiastically to the Grecian system of education, intellectual and physical, says, "Now, if the promoters of higher education for women will teach girls not only to understand the Greek tongue, but to copy somewhat of the Greek physical training; of that 'music and gymnastic' which helped to make the cleverest race of the Old World, the ablest race likewise, then they will earn the gratitude of the patriot and the physiologist, by doing their best to stay the downward tendencies of the physique, and therefore ultimately of the *morale*, in the coming generation of English women "

PART SECOND.

In referring to the history of the practical introduction of gymnastic training into schools, the countries of Europe, where this study has been making constant headway during the last half-century, naturally claim our first attention.

You will not be surprised to hear that during this time, as at the present day, the education of boys in this respect has received a larger share of thought and favor, from governments and from the public, than that of girls. It must, however, be borne in mind, that this is by no means because students of the subject have considered that girls are not in need of physical training. On the contrary, it has been everywhere distinctly understood and expressed, that it is partly on account of the claims of the army, and partly because, from their organization and habits, they repay better a certain kind of physical training, that the boys have received superior advantages.

Speaking roughly, there are three well-recognized systems of gymnastics, all of them at least half a century old, that, pure or mixed, are in use over most of the Continent of Europe at the present day.

1 The system of Frederick Jahn, born in Germany in 1778, which was framed rather to create athletes and soldiers, than to answer the more generally useful ends of physical culture, especially so far as girls are concerned. Its general adoption in Prussia and Denmark has, in fact, fairly helped to keep the claims of girls far in the background.

2. That of the Swede, Ling, born in 1776, who developed more fully than any one the free exercises of the body and limbs, performed with little or no apparatus, such as are now everywhere more or less in use, striving also, with zeal that rather overreached itself, to place his system upon a physiological basis.

3. That of Spiers in South Germany, born in 1810, who, working with unbounded personal enthusiasm, studied particularly the exercises requiring the concerted action of a number of persons These exercises found their full development in a sort of drill without arms, although freer movements, such as those of various dances, were also represented in them

It was my original intention to present some details of these different systems before you; but as this paper has already occupied so much time, and as they would be scarcely intelligible except to special teachers of this branch, I have thought it best to omit them I do not, indeed, feel myself able to discuss their comparative merits fairly; and I do not believe the time has arrived when it is important for us to do so.

If we look at the now prevailing condition of gymnastic instruction for girls in Europe, we find it to be as follows —

In Holland gymnastics are not taught in the primary schools in the country towns, but are taught at all schools in the large cities, in large halls kept for the purpose This instruction is given to both boys and girls None but the eldest classes use exercises that require apparatus of any kind. Instructors in gymnastics, both male and female, have abundant opportunity to fit themselves at the general normal schools, which are supported wholly or in part by government; and the male teachers are obliged to have passed an examination, theoretical and practical, in that branch. Furthermore, in order to supplement the efforts of government, a society called " Society for the Public Welfare" has instituted schools for gymnastics at several of the large cities, — Groningen, Amsterdam, Rotterdam, &c.

In Denmark gymnastics have been an obligatory study since 1814, both at the normal and at the general schools; and at Copenhagen there is a special institute for the instruction of professors of gymnastics This institute is under military charge, and its spirit is felt everywhere. The exercises have, however, a military turn

In Sweden the celebrated system of Ling is an obligatory study in all the public schools, three to six hours a week being devoted to it, subject to the advice of a physician who is appointed to examine each scholar at the beginning of the school term. For the education of teachers there is a great central institute at Stockholm; and the graduates from the normal schools must moreover have passed a special examination in this branch A former pupil of this Swedish system has established a gymnasium at Boston recently, and has taught also at the Girls' High School with excellent results, as far as could be judged in so short a time. A large part of the instruction is in the so-called "free exercises," including proper methods of sitting, standing, lying, walking, running, jumping, as well as exercises in concert, games, &c. The aim of these free exercises is to call into action in turn, the greater part of the voluntary muscles of the body; and with an intelligent, earnest teacher to direct them, there is no end to the modifications and combinations that can be made, calling for precision and strict attention and skill on the part of the pupils. As in all other exercises, the consciousness of progress made toward a good which still remains always in advance is always found to be attended with a sense of pleasure; and, the better the pupils are required to perform the exercises, the more they enjoy them.

In Prussia gymnastic culture has been obligatory in the primary schools, and indeed throughout Germany, in the schools for boys, is almost everywhere an obligatory study, although, except in the large cities, it is not systematically pursued. The official manual is a little book written by Angerstein, the Chief of the Municipal Normal School of Gymnastics of Berlin. The fact, that the importance is recognized of having the instruction in the branch systematic and thorough, is shown by the care which is taken to provide abundantly for the instruction of teachers

At Berlin, for example, three different varieties of diploma of professor of gymnastics are conferred. These are. 1. The diploma of the Central Institute, or its equivalent, that of the Municipal Normal School, or of a special examining commission, which gives the right, to instruct in the schools and seminaries of the higher grades throughout the State. 2. The diploma of those normal schools in which the study of gymnastics has been obligatory since 1854. This diploma constitutes a recommendation for its holder in seeking a place at any of the large schools of the city 3. The ordinary instruction diploma, accompanied with a certificate that its holder has followed a certain course of instruction in gymnastics at one of the normal schools, and is fitted to teach it among his other duties at any small school in the city or country. The examination for the higher diplomas is written, practical, and oral, requiring a knowledge of the various methods of instruction, the literature and history of the subject, and the rules for the construction of the apparatus, &c.

In Prussia, in striking contrast to the excessive attention paid by the government to the gymnastic training of boys, little or nothing has been done for the girls except through private means. Thus, out of a population of thirty-nine thousand girls at Berlin, seventeen hundred and forty-five only, or four and a half per cent from nine schools, received any degree of instruction in 1873 That this neglect has not been due to a want of appreciation of the importance of physical training for girls, is shown by the simple fact, that when in 1864 the Gymnastic Society of Berlin, supported by a recognized medical commission, petitioned the Minister of Education to initiate some changes in this respect, they were answered, that although fully appreciating the necessity of gymnastic training for girls and ready to encourage private efforts to obtain it, the government was unwilling to take the initiatory steps Manifestly the needs of the army was a stronger influence with it than the desire to improve the general physical culture of the people.

It will be remembered, that in the early part of this paper I said that attention had been called to this point in Berlin, at a recent meeting of teachers of the higher girls' schools; and I may add that, after the discussion, an officer of the government stated that changes were already in prospect in the organization of the Great Central Institute for teachers at Berlin, favoring the education of female teachers in this branch. In this connection another point may be mentioned which directly interests us; viz, the habit, both in Prussia and Holland and other places, of encouraging the study of physical culture among actual teachers in the schools by giving them opportunity of attending closely, during three or four weeks in each year, to gymnastic courses at some good institution, the government supplying their places while absent, and even paying their expenses.

In other provinces of Germany, more is done in the way of instruction for girls, mainly in the shape of courses for which a small fee is paid, such instruction is given under the auspices of that great gymnastic confederation which extends all over Germany, counting more than a hundred and fifty thousand members, and serving to keep alive a love of physical culture throughout the land.

In England there is no obligatory instruction in this branch, but earnest appeals have been made for its introduction.

In France, Austria, and Switzerland, it is made obligatory by laws which, in the two latter countries at least, are thoroughly carried into execution. Of the capital of Austria we have already spoken in an earlier part of the paper

In Switzerland, the importance of the subject is fully recognized; and the study of gymnastics is, nominally at least, obligatory Here also military drill, the merits of which as compared with other kinds of physical training I shall not now discuss, is very much in vogue.

Of the history of physical training in this country, I need not speak at length. It is true that something has been done by general regulation in certain places, — for instance, in Boston, where at this moment a rule exists that a few minutes of each half-session in the public schools should be devoted to physical exercise; but systematic attention to the subject pushed to the point of success has been due to private enterprise.

The number of these individual instances, however, and the degree of their success, have been great enough to warrant the conclusion that under proper auspices it would be both practicable and useful to introduce physical training as an obligatory study more generally into our schools, as may be seen from the remarks in the paper on school hygiene by Dr. F. Winsor, in the report of the Massachusetts State Board of Health, of January, 1874   The most notable cases of success that have come to my knowledge have occurred in the Boston schools during the period of Prof Monroe's teaching, though he directed his attention particularly to the cultivation of the voice; at Vassar College, at the State Normal School at Philadelphia; and at Amherst; not to speak of the many schools where gymnastics have been used to a greater or less extent, nor of the public and private teaching of Dr. Dio Lewis, Dr Mason, and others   The example set by Amherst College is peculiarly instructive.   It is now a dozen years since a number of gentlemen, officers and friends of the college, solved in the affirmative the question as to whether or not a system of light gymnastics, to be practised daily, could be made at once interesting and beneficial to college students of an age when a revolt against irksome and tedious tasks is most in order.   The system is established now on a firm basis; and the founders can point with pride to the testimony of graduates and undergraduates, and to a diminished sick-list, in proof of the success of their undertaking.

Yet their materials are of the simplest order, consisting of a piano and wooden dumb-bells; and their exercises are invented by themselves. They have, of course, had their slight ups and downs, from time to time, and have come to some interesting conclusions, one of which is, that the accompaniment of music is a *sine qua non* of the success of the enterprise.

PART THIRD.

In recommending the adoption of a practical system of gymnastics in our own schools, there remains but little more for me to say.   All authorities agree, that teachers skilled in the work, and convinced of its importance, are necessary to the success of any system.   We must, then, endeavor to obtain a large number of good teachers; and these would naturally be drawn from the normal schools; and with them lies, to some extent, the key to the situation   A sufficient number of teachers, for these schools at least, could be obtained either from abroad or at home, — for example, graduates of the schools and colleges already mentioned, and others like them, — as has already been done to a certain extent   The final aim would be to fit all teachers for giving instruction in this branch; and a step in this direction might be taken, by making arrangements by which teachers could leave their schools for two or three weeks at a time, in order to attend gymnastic courses.

As to the system itself, it seems to me, that there should be exercises of some sort once or twice daily, for a few moments only, as is largely done already; and, two or three times a week, more extended instruction be given.   If, at the same time, a fondness for physical culture could be made to spread from the teacher among the pupils, and from them again among the public, much good might be indirectly accomplished.   The conclusions arrived at by the Belgian Commission, so often referred to, are very interesting in this connection   They review with some care the comparative merits of the system in which fixed apparatus is employed, and that in which none or very little such is used, and give their opinions in favor of the latter, at the same time specifying with minuteness exactly what pieces of movable or fixed apparatus they consider permissible.

They condemn the complicated systems in use in many places, which have for their aim, the acquiring of great strength, and the power to perform athletic feats, as objectionable and impracticable; and quote the opinions of gymnasts and experts as to the great value of the free exercises; and recommend lastly, that these exercises should be practised twice daily, and directed by the teachers at large, who should receive their instruction at normal schools, where the subject should be made obligatory.   Whatever be the merits of any practical system, however, it must fail of accomplishing its object, if not nourished and supported by the conviction and enthusiasm of its teachers and the public.

Inasmuch as greater weight is attached to the testimony of practical workers in any field, than to that of theorizers only, I shall ask your attention for a moment to a few extracts of letters, from teachers of high rank, in various parts of the country, upon the subject with which we have been dealing   From a distant State one writes, —

"They (physical exercises) should not only have a place in the daily programme, but their observance should be as regular as that of any other exercise   The tendency of the system of graded schools is to limit the work done, to the course definitely laid down in the several grades, and to limit it still further within this course to those topics which are made the subject of examination in passing from one grade to another   In teaching these, the teacher expends largely his time and energy   Now, as physical exercise has not been placed on a level with the scholastic work of the school, made compulsory to all, and a condition to promotion, it has not generally received regular and systematic attention. Our schools are, in the main, shaped by public sentiment, and do move efficiently much in advance of popular opinion, as represented by the school-officers of the country."

The principal of a "girls' normal school" in one of the large cities writes, —

"The most extraordinary results have been produced. Before the introduction of this subject (physical culture), the exceptions to the rule were those who did not have the headache: now the exceptions are those who do have have it Upon examination, we have found that systematic instruction in this direction necessarily breaks up the injurious habit of tight lacing, from the fact that the pupils must wear loose dresses upon those days set apart for practice; and the consequence is, healthy, vigorous, rosy-cheeked girls."

Miss——, who has managed this department of the school just mentioned, "with great success for several years," writes, "There is, I am sorry to say, a deplorable lack of interest here, as elsewhere, in the subject of physical education, . . . while our future men and women, forced to sit by the hour with cramped muscles and contracted chests, in schoolrooms where the air is foul with many breaths, will graduate quite probably with active minds, but almost certainly with enervated, undeveloped bodies. . . . There is but one public school in this neighborhood at the present time, where there is a department of physical education conducted upon these conditions (persistent systematic training). . . . To establish such a department, demands but little change in the present school system, since almost any schoolroom may be transformed almost instantaneously into a gymnasium, no apparatus being required for the lower grades, and only a few light implements carried in the hands for the more advanced pupils, and each scholar needing only space enough upon the floor for a step in each direction, and room to straighten the arms in front and at the sides Of the pupils, the requirement is slight, being merely that the dress shall be short enough to leave the feet unencumbered, loose enough to admit of a full inhalation without feeling the clothes at the waist or across the chest, and large enough to permit the free play of every muscle in the body. For this, no special costume would be required, except in the highest grades Music is a great addition to the exercise, but not a necessity. But the great difficulty, and in fact the only serious one, is the dearth of regularly trained teachers of gymnastics, who are not only fully prepared for the work, but who are enthusiastic in the cause, and able to impart their information to others. This arises from the low standard of physical culture admitted by public opinion. Let it once be required, that those who teach this branch shall of necessity be regularly trained, and there will be a supply of good teachers in a marvellously short time."

The principal of the school last referred to touches, as it seems to me, upon a point of greatest practical importance when he says that the introduction of light gymnastics into his school has done something toward initiating a real reform in the dress of the girls Enough is said in these days of the evil results that follow upon tight lacing and the wearing of dresses which do not admit of the free use of the arms; and yet the practical work of conversion goes on but slowly if, however, the rules of the school obliged the girls to wear a more reasonable dress two or three times a week when the exercises were performed, it might fairly be expected that the real merits would be recognized and remembered. The arguments of comfort are stronger than those of persuasion.

In conclusion I wish to make mention of a few of the best books upon gymnastic training, in order that it may be seen how much attention the subject has attracted in different parts of the world, and the direction in which its supporters are working. The first of which I shall speak is a closely printed book of about four hundred pages, called "Statistik und Schul-Turners in Deutschland" (Statistics of Gymnastic Instruction in the Schools of Germany), published by the National Turnerschaft in 1874, and giving accurate statistics of the extent to which gymnastics is actually practised in every school throughout Germany and Austria. It contains, besides, an apparently complete statement of the German literature on the subject, comprising more than a hundred books, together with a variety of other facts compiled with the precision in which German statistical works are known to excel.

Another notable work is the "Theoretisches Handbuch fur Turner," by Angerstein, director of the Stadtische Turnhalle in Berlin It is made up mainly by lectures given by him in his course for the instruction of teachers. It treats of the elements of human anatomy and physiology, the history of the use of gymnastics among the ancients, and its introduction into Europe, as well as the practical details of a manual. The subject of gymnastics for girls is thoroughly discussed in a book of four hundred pages by Herr Kloss, who holds in Dresden a similar position to that of Angerstein in Berlin. Another excellent and similar work upon the same subject was published in 1872 by Schettler, a director in Plauen; and in both of them a good deal of space is given to the description of games to be played out of doors, many of them accompanied with songs of which the music is given. The æsthetic side of the subject is presented in a book, among others, upon the Gymnastic Culture of the Greeks, by Otto Yager.

Of the books in the French language, I will mention only the "Gymnastique Populaire Raisonné," by Junot and Sanglet, published in Neufchâtel in 1873; of those in English, two books by Archibald MacLaren of the Oxford gymnasium, meant rather for colleges than schools; several by Matthias Roth of London; and in this country the well-known books by Dr. Dio Lewis, who writes with vigor of the importance of gymnastic instruction, and gives some exercises invented by himself; and the manual by Prof. Monroe of Boston, already mentioned.

The manual of exercises in use at Amherst, invented largely by its author, Prof. E H. Barlow of 1866, the captain of their gymnastic class, has also been published. A more detailed account of these works will not now be necessary. Enough has been said to show the spirit in which the subject has been approached by experts; and those who wish to give it more careful study will find the materials ready to their hands.

At the session for discussing the Effects of School Life upon the Eyes of Children, a paper was read by Dr. Webster of New York, embodying the statistical results of the investigations now in progress under the direction of Dr. C. R. Agnew. The work is still incomplete, and will doubtless require one year more, at the least, before it can be published as a whole The following is from an abstract of the paper, made by Dr. Agnew : —

EXAMINATIONS OF THE EYES OF AMERICAN SCHOOL CHILDREN.

European observers have demonstrated the fact, that during school-life there are developed in the eyes of scholars, diseases which increase in frequency and gravity from the primary to the university grades. It is not necessary to repeat here a review of the work of Cohn, Erismann, and others, as that has already been done elsewhere. Our object now is, to begin a statement of the result of preliminary examinations made in New York, Brooklyn and Cincinnati, on the same subject. In these cities, the eyes of scholars, 2,884 in number (the eyes, and not the scholars, are enumerated, as there is frequently a difference between the two eyes of one person), of both sexes, ranging in age from six to twenty-six years, were examined, and the conditions as to the refraction and diseases noted and tabulated. In the same connection, the state of the schoolrooms as to light, desks, heating, and ventilation was observed; as also the length and distribution of study-hours, and other facts affecting health.

In Cincinnati, O , 1,264 eyes of scholars were examined by Dr. Ayers and Dr. D Booth Williams. About one-third of these belonged to the district schools, one-third to the intermediate, and the remaining third to the normal and high schools. In the district schools, 13 3 per cent were near-sighted (11.3 of the boys, and 15 3 of the girls). In the intermediate schools, 13.8 per cent were near-sighted (9 5 per cent of the boys, and 18 1 per cent of the girls). In the normal and high schools, 22 8 per cent were near-sighted (22.2 per cent of the boys, and 23.2 per cent of the girls)

Dr. J. S. Prout and Dr. Arthur Mathewson examined 600 eyes of students at the Polytechnic, Brooklyn, N.Y., all boys, 284 belonging to the academic, and 316 to the collegiate department. In the academic department, 9.2 per cent were near-sighted, and in the collegiate department 21.8 per cent were near-sighted. Dr. William Cheatham examined 1,020 eyes of students in the New York College, New York, all boys; 670 belonging to the introductory class, 210 to the Freshmen, 110 to the Sophomores, and 30 to the Juniors. In the introductory class, which is made up entirely of students who have passed the public schools, 21.9 per cent were near-sighted; of the eyes of Freshmen, 26.2 per cent were near-sighted; of the Sophomores, 22.7 per cent were near-sighted; of the Juniors examined, 50 per cent were near-sighted. The number of Juniors examined was too small, however, to be of any scientific value.

The tables show that *staphyloma posticum*, one of the gravest organic changes in progressive near-sightedness, increased from 0.5 per cent in the district schools, to 7.6 per cent in the intermediate, and 10.4 per cent in the normal and high schools.

The following paper was presented, but not read, at the same session: —

RULES FOR THE CARE OF THE EYES.

BY DR. D. F. LINCOLN, SECRETARY OF THE DEPARTMENT OF HEALTH,

When writing, reading, drawing, sewing, &c., always take care that

(*a.*) The room is comfortably cool, and the feet warm;

(*b.*) There is nothing tight about the neck;

(*c.*) There is plenty of light, without dazzling the eyes;

(*d.*) The sun does not shine directly on the object we are at work upon;

(*e.*) The light does not come from in front: it is best when it comes over the left shoulder;

(*f.*) The head is not very much bent over the work;

(*g.*) The page is nearly perpendicular to the line of sight; that is, that the eye is nearly opposite the middle of the page, for an object held slanting is not seen so clearly;

(*h.*) That the page, or other object, is not less than fifteen inches from the eye.

Nearsightedness is apt to increase rapidly when a person wears, in reading, the glasses intended to enable him to see distant objects.

In any case, when the eyes have any defect, avoid fine needlework, drawing of fine maps, and all such work, except for very short tasks, not exceeding half an hour each, and in the morning.

Never study or write before breakfast by candle-light.

Do not lie down when reading.

If your eyes are aching from firelight, from looking at the snow, from overwork, or other causes, a pair of colored glasses may be advised, to be used for a while. Light blue or grayish blue is the best shade; but these glasses are likely to be abused, and usually are not to be worn, except under medical advice. Almost all those persons who continue to wear colored glasses, having, perhaps, first received advice to wear them from medical men, would be better without them. Travelling vendors of spectacles are not to be trusted: their wares are apt to be recommended as ignorantly and indiscriminately as in the times of the " Vicar of Wakefield."

If you have to hold the pages of " Harper's Magazine " nearer than fifteen inches in order to read it easily, it is probable that you are quite nearsighted. If you have to hold it two or three feet away before you see easily, you are probably farsighted. In either case, it is very desirable to consult a physician before getting a pair of glasses, for a *misfit* may permanently injure your eyes.

Never play tricks with the eyes, as squinting or rolling them.

The eyes are often troublesome when the stomach is out of order.

Avoid reading or sewing by twilight, or when debilitated by recent illness, especially fever.[1]

Every seamstress ought to have a cutting-out table to place her work on such a plane with reference to the line of vision as to make it possible to exercise a close scrutiny without bending the head or the figure much forward.

Usually, except for aged persons or chronic invalids, the winter temperature in workrooms ought not to exceed 60° or 65°. To sit with impunity in a room at a lower temperature, some added clothing will be necessary. The feet of a student or seamstress should be kept comfortably warm while tasks are being done. Slippers are bad. In winter the temperature of the lower part of the room is apt to be 10° or 15° lower than that of the upper.

It is indispensable, in all forms of labor requiring the exercise of vision or minute objects, that the worker should rise from his task now and then, take a few deep inspirations with closed mouth, stretch the frame out into the most erect posture, throw the arms backward and forward, and, if possible, step to a window or into the open air, if only for a moment. Two desks or tables in a room are valuable for a student, — one to stand at, the other to sit at.

The next subject of discussion was the establishment of the office of Medical Inspector of Public Schools. It was opened by reading the brief of a State law, prepared by Joseph Willard, Esq., of Boston, modelled essentially upon the Massachusetts law establishing the State Board of Health. It is here printed, not as a measure which receives in every point the sanction of the Department of Health, but as containing many valuable features.

PROJECT OF A LAW ESTABLISHING THE OFFICE OF MEDICAL INSPECTOR OF SCHOOLS.

First, He shall be appointed by the head of the Department of Public Instruction.

Second, Term of office three years.

Third, Must be a physician

Fourth, Is expected to devote his entire time to the duties of this office.

Fifth, Salary three thousand dollars, payable quarterly, plus necessary expenses for clerical labor and travel.

Sixth, He shall take cognizance of the interests of health among the eachers and children of the public schools.

Seventh, He shall make sanitary investigations in respect to schoolhouses

[1] Or in the case of women, by childbirth.

and grounds, and to all circumstances connected with the management and instruction of schools, which may appear to influence the health of scholars or .teachers.

Eighth, He shall make himself acquainted with the means employed in other States for preserving the health of the inmates of schools.

Ninth, He shall seek to trace the origin and mode of extension of epidemic or other diseases among inmates of schools, and to point out measures for the arrest or prevention of such diseases.

Tenth, He shall from time to time inform the Department of Public Instruction of the results of the aforesaid investigations, and shall suggest to the said department such modifications of the system of instruction and management existing in the schools of this State, as, in his opinion, would conduce to the improvement of the health of teachers and scholars.

Eleventh, He shall further, in the month of January of every year, present to the Department of Public Instruction a written report of his doings and investigations in the line of his duty as aforsesaid for the year ending with the 31st of December next preceding.

Twelfth, He shall gather, and from time to time shall present to the department, such information, in respect to the interests of the public schools as he may deem proper for diffusion among the people.

The concluding session of the Department, held May 13, was occupied by accounts of the Philadelphia examinations, and of those instituted by Prof. Bowditch; these have already been spoken of on p. 86. A paper containing a synopsis of the leading principles in school architecture was also read, and occasioned much comment. It is not reproduced here. The session adjourned at noon, *sine die,* after passing a vote of thanks to the chairman, Rev. Mr. Brigham.

SPECIAL PAPERS

OF THE

SOCIAL SCIENCE ASSOCIATION.

PRODUCTION AND DISTRIBUTION OF WEALTH. By DAVID A. WELLS. An address read at Detroit, May 11, 1875. (22 pages.) Single copies 20 cents. $1 per dozen.

THE WORK OF SOCIAL SCIENCE, PAST AND PRESENT. By F. B. SANBORN. A report read at Detroit, May 12, 1875. (15 pages.) Single copies 10 cents. The same, in covers with Mr. Wells's address, 25 cents.

PROGRESS IN INTERNATIONAL LAW. By Pres. ANGELL of Michigan. (16 pages.) Single copies 20 cents.

HEALTH IN SCHOOLS. Papers and Reports of the Department of Health, Detroit, May, 1875. (48 pages.) Single copies 20 cents. $8.00 per dozen.

LEGAL EDUCATION IN THE NORTH-WEST. By Prof. W. G. HAMMOND. (12 pages.) Single copies 10 cents.

PROCEEDINGS OF THE CONFERENCE OF CHARITIES, AT DETROIT, May, 1875. (104 pages.) Single copies 50 cents. $5 per dozen.

TENT HOSPITALS. By J. FOSTER JENKINS, M. D. (24 pages, with illustrations.) Single copies 25 cents. $2.50 per dozen.

CONFERENCE OF BOARDS OF HEALTH AT NEW YORK. (50 pages.) Single copies 25 cents. $2.50 per dozen.

CONFERENCE OF BOARDS OF CHARITIES, 1874. (52 pages.) Single copies 25 cents. $2.00 per dozen.

GENERAL MEETING AT DETROIT, 1875. (20 pages, with Constitution and list of Members of the Association.) Single copies 15 cents. $1.50 per dozen.

PAUPERISM IN NEW YORK. By C. L. BRACE. (16 pages.) Single copies 10 cents. $1 per dozen. $5 per hundred.

RATIONAL PRINCIPLES OF TAXATION. By D. A. WELLS. (14 pages.) Single copies 10 cents. $1 per dozen.

OCEAN LANES FOR STEAMSHIPS. By Prof. PEIRCE, Capt. FORBES, and Com. WYMAN. (13 pages.) Single copies 10 cents. $1 per dozen.

THE FARMERS' MOVEMENT IN THE WEST. By W. C. FLAGG. (16 pages.) Single copies 10 cents. $1 per dozen.

AMERICAN RAILROADS. By GARDINER G. HUBBARD. (12 pages.) Single copies 10 cents. $1 per dozen.

AMERICAN FINANCE. By Prof. W. G. SUMNER. (11 pages.) Single copies 10 cents. $1 per dozen.

PRIVATE PROPERTY UPON THE SEA. By Rev. Dr. WOOLSEY. (20 pages.) Single copies 15 cents. $1.50 per dozen.

Other SPECIAL PAPERS appearing in the *Journal of Social Science* may be ordered separately, when in print, at the rate of 10 cents for every fifteen pages.

The above pamphlets, and all the other publications of the American Social Science Association, including Nos. 2, 3, 5, 6, 7, and 8 of the Journal of Social Science, may be ordered of the publishers

A. WILLIAMS & CO.,

283 WASHINGTON ST., BOSTON;

G. P. PUTNAM'S SONS, NEW YORK; PORTER & COATES, PHILADELPHIA;
ROBERT CLARKE & CO., CINCINNATI;

Or of the Secretary of the Association, 5 Pemberton Square Boston.

PUBLICATIONS

OF THE

American Social Science Association.

A Handbook for Immigrants to the United States. 1 vol., crown 8vo, linen, 50 cts. CONTENTS.—Part I. General Directions—Part II. The United States—Part III. The State—Part IV. The Territories—Part V. The Public Lands.

Collections of Casts. Subjects selected for the Girls' High and Normal School, Boston; the mode and cost of procuring them; with an additional list of subjects. Pamphlet, crown 8vo, paper, 15 cts.

Free Public Libraries. Suggestions on their foundation and administration; with a selected list of books. Crown 8vo, pamphlet, 25 cts. Revised edition now ready.

Journal of Social Science. Containing the Transactions of the American Association. Nos. I.–V., 8vo, paper, $1.50. Nos. VI., VII., VIII., each $1.00,

CONTENTS OF NUMBER TWO.—Current Record of the Association—I. Immigration. Friedrich Kapp—II. The American Census, James A. Garfield—III. The Mode of Procedure in Cases of Contested Elections. Henry L. Dawes—IV. The Public Charities of the State of New York. Theodore W. Dwight—V. The Public Libraries of the United States. Ainsworth R. Spofford—VI. The Science of Disappointing. Joseph B. Potts—VII. Vaccination. A Report presented by Francis Bacon, William A. Hammond, and David F. Lincoln—VIII. The Election of Presidents. Charles Francis Adams, Jun.—IX. Life Insurance. Sheppard Homans—X. The Administration of Criminal Justice. George C. Barrett—XI. Health Laws and their Administration. Elisha Harris—XII. An International Code. D. D. Field XIII. General Intelligence—XIV. Constitution—XV. List of New Members—XVI. List of Works relating to Social Science published in 1869.

CONTENTS OF NUMBER THREE.—I. Public Parks and the Enlargement of Towns. F. L. Olmsted—II. Art Education in America. C. C. Perkins—III. Civilization and Health. Francis Bacon—IV. American System of Patents. S. A. Duncan—V. Natural Sphere of Police Power. T. D. Woolsey—VI. Legislation and Social Science. E. L. Godkin—VII. Representation of Minorities. D. B. Field—VIII. Relations of Business Men to National Legislation. H. A. Hill—IX. Houses in the Country for Working Men. G. B. Emerson—X. Minority Representation in Europe. Thomas Hare—XI. Application of Mr. Hare's System of Voting to the Nomination of Overseers of Harvard College. W. R. Ware—XII. General Intelligence: 1. Home; 2. Foreign.

NUMBER FOUR is out of print, as well as NUMBER ONE.

CONTENTS OF NUMBER FIVE.—I. Municipal Government. Dorman B. Eaton—II. Higher Education of Woman. T. W. Higginson—III. Restoration of the Currency. Joseph S. Ropes—IV. Small Result of the Census. Francis A. Walker—V. Public Vaccination. J. P. Foster—VI. The International. David A. Wasson—VII. Legislation in Relation to Pharmacy. G. F. B. Markoe—VIII. General Intelligence.

CONTENTS OF NUMBER SIX.—General Meeting at New York—I. Opening Address. George William Curtis—II. The Work of Social Science in the United States. F. B. Sanborn—III. Financial Administration. G. Bradford—IV. Conference of Boards of Public Charities—V. Pauperism in the City of New York—VI. The Farmers' Movement in the Western States. Willard C. Flagg—VII. Ocean Lanes for Steamship Navigation. Prof. B. Peirce—VIII. Railroad Principles of Legislation. David A. Wells—IX. American Railroads. Gardiner G. Hubbard—X. Reformation of Prisons. Z. R. Brockway—XI. The Deaf-Mute College at Washington. Edward M. Gallaudet—XII. The Protection of Animals. George T. Angell—XIII. American Finance. Prof. W. G. Sumner.

CONTENTS OF NUMBER SEVEN.—I. Private Property and the Son. Rev. Dr. Woolsey—II. Conference of Boards of Health—III. School Hygiene. Dr. D. F. Lincoln and A. D. C. Twill—IV. The Hospitals. Dr. J. F. Jenkins—V. National, State, and Harvard Universities. A. D. White and D. C. Gilman—VI. Free Lending Libraries. W. W. Greenough—VII. The Young Men's Christian Associations. Cephas Brainard—VIII. Prison Reform in Europe and America. The. Wines and F. B. Sanborn—X. Social Science Record—XI. Conference of Boards of Charities.

CONTENTS OF NUMBER EIGHT.—I. The Production and Distribution of Wealth. David A. Wells—II. The Work of Social Science. F. B. Sanborn—III. Progress in International Law. J. A. Angell—IV. The Experiment of Civil Service Reform. Dorman B. Eaton—V. The Treatment of the Insane. W. G. Eliot—VI. Health in Schools. Dr. D. F. Lincoln—J. Putnam, &c.—VII. Financial Policy of England and the United States. VIII. Limitations of Judicial Power. Emory Washburn—IX. Life Insurance for the Poor. Elizur Wright and Sheppard Homans—X. Legal Education. W. G. Hammond—XI. The Detroit Meeting.

Sent free of expense, on receipt of the price annexed, by the Publishers.

A. WILLIAMS & CO., Boston.   G. P. PUTNAM'S SONS, New York.
   ROBERT CLARKE & CO., Cincinnati.   PORTER & COATES, Philadelphia.

Or by the Secretary of the Association, 5 Pemberton Sq., Boston.

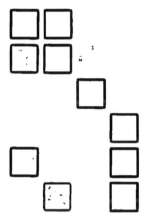

Lightning Source UK Ltd.
Milton Keynes UK
UKHW022334060223
416579UK00001B/39